Civil Poems

Gabriel Trujillo Muñoz

Translated by
José María Mantero and Phillip Dunn

Spuyten Duyvil
New York City

ISBN 978-1-959556-94-7
cover art : t thilleman

Library of Congress Control Number: 2023952275

for Uberto Stabile,
who saw the frontier as the land of poetry

Big will not always be big
Nor will the small always be small

Bertolt Brecht

No-one is forgotten
Nothing is forgotten

Olga Bergholz

I was then with my people
where my people, unfortunately, were

Anna Akhmatova

Contents

PROLOGUE
José María Mantero

Through his innovative use of the fantasy, science fiction, and crime fiction genres as well as his poetry, essays, and short story collections, Gabriel Trujillo Muñoz has brought attention to social, political, and economic challenges faced by the nation and the people of México. Frequently, the setting for his works is the border between the United States and México and, more specifically, the region of Baja, California, and the city of Mexicali. As Trujillo Muñoz wrote in his collection of essays *Cruzar / Mudar / Permanecer. La filosofía de la frontera y sus pensamientos nómadas* (2012) (*Crossing / Moving / Remaining. Border Philosophy and Nomad Thinking*), "the border where I live is an endless sandbank, a hard and hostile land complete in its living and resilient nature, in its healing and translucid light; it is a barbed wire fence, a corrugated tin wall, an anvil of second-hand objects, and a city, like Mexicali, that is a mirage in the middle of the desert" (117) (Our translation).

When in 2013 I presented a conference in English on his work *Espantapájaros* (2013) (*Scarecrow*) and subsequently expanded this paper and published it as an article in 2018, I remember thinking what a challenge it would be to translate this novel and offer this unique perspective on cross-border dynamics to an English-speaking audience. Although this did not come to fruition, in 2016 Phillip Dunn and I embarked upon a translation of *Poemas civiles—Civil Poems—*, a collection of poems that addresses the poverty, corruption, and violence of contemporary México and beyond. As Trujillo Muñoz indicates in the End Note to this volume, "I wrote these poems because I do not accept the normalcy of violence, the charade of impunity, the pretext of ignorance. I wrote them to say what I think and what I feel as a Mexican in a nation that is falling apart day by day, where inequality and injustice are growing by leaps and bounds and with the permission of those who have the most."

If translation is, in effect, an exercise in futility, it would seem that a translator's responsibility is to tackle that futility, to reconcile the impossible task of finding exact linguistic and lexical correspondences with offering an alternative and acceptable iteration. Therein lies the value of translation: to bridge these extremes, to both accept and transcend the variances, creating, in the process, a new text, one that is ever beholden to the original. In the case of *Civil Poems,* we approached the individual poems as readers, exchanging semantic and thematic impressions and word choices and reconsidering conundrums. The second poem in the collection, "Survivors," is a case in point. In English, the title itself is relatively straightforward and, as we read in the poem, refers to those who, in México today, are surviving the endemic violence and corruption, yet, paradoxically, are lost and struggling to keep their heads above water. Although in Spanish the two possibilities, *sobreviviente* and *superviviente*, are practically synonymous, Trujillo Muñoz chose *superviviente* for the title. Although subtle, the choice of this term instead of *sobreviviente* and the presence of the prefix *super-* imbues the subject of the poem—those who continue to survive in today's México—with heroic qualities that, in truth, do little to dispel the profound sense of loss and confusion. Our translation of this poem, then, encouraged us to invoke this everyday heroism and confusion while, at the same time, remaining faithful to the spirit and letter of the text. "What are we now?", that question repeated at the beginning of practically every stanza of "Survivors," defines the deep uncertainty and search for something that will transcend the moment. The final response and subsequent conclusion of the poem's translation in English, "Darkness passing / Aimless through the night," approaches the original Spanish, "*El paso de las tinieblas / Por la noche sin rumbo.*" However, the logical word order and positioning of the verse in Spanish keeps the reader in a state of suspended expectation, as *tinieblas*—that "darkness"—arrives only at the end of the line. "*El paso*" ("the passing"), it begins, and we ask, *de qué*, of what? Only at the end is the answer revealed, "*de *las tinieblas"* ("of darkness"). That *"tinieblas"* that ends the line in the original Spanish and holds the reader in a state of anticipation became, in our translation, the beginning: "Darkness passing." In our reading, the "darkness passing" saturates the subjects of the poem—those everyday Mexicans—with the capacity to weather the "passing of darkness." By positioning the term "darkness" as the first word of the final stanza, an attempt is made to draw attention to both the current state of affairs in México (that "darkness") and the courage to survive it.

Each translated poem could be described and considered in this way, to within an inch of its textual death. For the inspiration to decode these texts and transform them into something quite possibly unintended by their author, we are deeply indebted to Gabriel Trujillo Muñoz. His vision of contemporary México and continuous forays into its past, present, and possible certain futures through poetry, fiction, and non-fiction lead, in both Spanish and English, to a better understanding of the relationship between the United States and México and of the challenges faced by the people of México.

LUBYANKA REVISITED

In front of the doors of the prison of Lubyanka
An old woman recognized the poet Ana Akhmatova
Who was visiting her son
      Imprisoned on Stalin's orders.

"Can you tell what is happening here?"
Asked the old woman in a whisper

"I can,"
Answered the poet.

And the old woman smiled slightly in triumph
For if someone remembers the tragedy
The authorities cannot silence it completely
For if someone recounts the horror
Those who endured it will not have suffered in vain

Will we then
At the doors of our own Lubyanka
Arm ourselves with courage to speak out?
At the silent walls of the power that surround us
Will we together be able to tell what happens here?
Will we have the courage not to forget this war: this debacle: this rip?

SURVIVORS

What are we now?
The wayward sons
Of a homeland adrift

What are we now?
The breath of history
In the maelstrom of time

What are we now?
The homeland in its bitterness
The nation in its perils

What are we now?
An immense ruin
A bloodstain

Darkness passing
Aimless through the night

THE FOUNDING MYTH

Then
In the year of the bloodied sun
The emperor of the Aztecs
Looked into the mirror of the gods
And contemplated the future to come.

His kingdom in flames
His people enslaved

When will this happen?
He asked with panic in his voice.

We know not
Answered the priests at his service
The mirror but reveals
That which each deposit in its reflection

The nightmares that each brings with him.

History of a Homeland

Once we were a dream
A promise barely sketched

Once we were a pact of loyalty
An embrace under the summer sun

Once we were a flag in the wind
A sound of sabers and machetes

Once we were a train station
A woman with a pistol at her waist

Once we were a pilgrimage
A familiar pasture in the Alameda

Once we were a march of protest
Amongst the soldiers' bayonets

Once we were a crowd
In the shadow of the skyscrapers

Once we were dream
A promise barely sketched

NATURAL DISASTERS

If the world sinks
Why were we stuck with a third-class ticket?

If the earth shudders
Who made us the ramparts?

If life becomes extinct
What teaching does it leave us?

Every day
We learn the lessons
That haunt our minds:
Fragile are we in the face of disaster
Peace is a space between two quakes
Each day a stumble: each pain a wound

HOUSE ON GUARD

The house has turned into a trench
A drawbridge
A ruthless frontier

The house has turned into a hideout
A refuge against the squall of time

While the lions
Wait patiently
For someone to make a wrong step

While the tigers prowl outside
With puffed-up chests
             Roaring

The house has become a prison
A cell where suspicion grows
Like a fungus in the shadows

A closed site
Where panic is
A heart bitten by anguish
An empty shell without an escape hatch

A house defended
Against the specters
That inhabit our days

A last defense
Against the ghosts
In their eager rage

In their endless thirst

Unspoiled and Sparkling

On the ninetieth anniversary of La suave patria[*]

No
           Ramón
Don't say it anymore:
We were never that country
Unspoiled and sparkling
Except in your poetry
Except in your nostalgia
For an inland homeland

No
           Ramón
Don't say it anymore:
That country was yours
In its mysteries
Like a wounded love
In the garden of memory
Like an angel of fire with the sky above

It's time to accept it:
This Mexico of ours
Is a somersault
An act of suicide

---

[*] La suave patria (1921) by Ramón López Velarde is one of the best known poems in
Mexican poetry. Its verses are a hymn to everyday life and proclaim the longing for a
quiet, traditional existence, far from the shocks and anguish of the Mexican Revolution,
which at that time was the storm that shook the country, tearing away customs and
habits, but it is also the discovery of an awakening society, the experience of new civic
freedoms. The homeland was, in this work, a cornucopia of longings to be realized, of
dreams to be fulfilled.

Under the beastly darkness
A lost song

Under the shadow of the world
A restless uproar
A carnivorous plant

MUNICIPAL PANTHEON: DAY OF THE DEAD

Nothing seems excessive
Out of place
In this city of stone
Where everything is festival and celebration
Weeping and boisterous

The children play
At cops and *narcos*
Among the abandoned tombs

The music of the mariachi sounds
With insistent persistence

The iron crosses
With their bundles of flowers
The marble statues
With their letters of gold
Give the stage its tone
The show its weight

Once in a while
Someone sobs
Someone draws his pistol
And fires into the air

So that the dead know
How much they are loved
So that the living can
Continue on their way

Calm
In peace

The Ballad of the Rotten Times

To those who tomorrow
Live in this land
To those who in the future
Are called Mexicans
Please do not remember us
Too harshly

We also
Wanted a just country
We also
Wished for a free homeland

And although we never protested
Against the gags on thinking
Against the idle pursuits of power
You should understand our situation:
We lived in gloomy times
In places where life was worth nothing

What did you expect us to do?
Die for a cause?
Sacrifice ourselves for our fellows?

Come on!
We were wretched: not suicidal
We were weak: not idiotic

We survived
Is that not our greatest heritage?
Is that not our best legacy?

Difficult Times

Hard days are coming
Difficult times
Said a German poet.

But that's
Old news
Around here.

Hard days
Difficult times
They're already here.

They live already,
A tempest of tempests
Among us.

TWENTY-FIRST CENTURY BIOGRAPHY

The country you're born in
A gamble

The country you live in
A spasm

The country you escape from
A torment

The country you come to
A riddle

There are no answers
For every action
And more than enough questions come out
When no one answers them

You've crossed borders
And now you don't know which country is yours
Which truth your name carries

Life is a smear on the landscape
A smudge without form or harmony

Mexican Zoology

Wolves
At their banquet

Hyenas
At their feast

Vultures
On high
Waiting their turn

HUNT

The smell of fear
Permeates our clothes

The carnage
Marks us
With its aroma

The beasts smell
Our tracks
In the distance

To them we are
Their favorite prey
Their scapegoat

Big Dog

Stuck on the wall
Is a poster
Of a man
With a frown
And an arrogant look

He is not even a demon:
He is a pet to amuse the bosses

He barks
So that they pay attention to him

He skips around
So that they throw him a bone

PROVERBS IN CIRCULATION

My blood: your blood
Every death is a natural death: even if they execute you
There's no betrayal if you're loyal to yourself
Even saints need bodyguards
We teach whoever messes with us to howl
Live good: live fast: die quickly
A body without a head sends a clear message
He who lives by the sword is dismembered by the sword
If they come for you they're coming for everybody
When the police nabs you let them take a picture: put on your best smile
If I like you: greasy food. If I don't like you: soup
To each his song: to each his exploits
Pray to Death: She'll always listen to you
Every territory has its owner: every old lady has hers
For every whore her beau: for every king his queen
The party's great if not even the neighbors complain
If you've got, it flaunt it: let them know your worth in gold
Eliminate your enemies and those who overshadow you: it's not good to
        hold a grudge
The boss is the boss: the rest of us are just workers
If you pay enough you can even buy the sky
The earth belongs to the one who razes it
The best part about this business is that they sing what you did: it's that
nobody forgets you
If you make it to twenty: you're good
If you make it to thirty: ruthless
If you make it to forty: cunning
If you make it to fifty: you're in prison
Your blood: my blood

SOMEONE SHOULD

Someone should sing
Of the ones no one sings of

Someone should preserve
What has already been forgotten

Someone should find
Among us
His epiphany

The Eden
Not subverted
By shrapnel

The paradise
Where no triumph
Is empty

THE HORROR

Just keep quiet
Just pay attention

Beneath the firefights
Beneath the calls for help
Behind the veil of the shouts and sirens
Something enormous
                    Colossal
Gives rhythm to all this paralysis

Just keep quiet
And you'll hear its pulse
The breakneck boom
Of the heart of darkness

Its heartbeat of bitter fever
Its sound of horror in crescendo

OSSUARY

I have nothing
Except my words
Which are not mine but everyone's

Words
To sing
Of life in its shock
Of death in its ascendance

This land was fertile land
I assure you

Here grew
The world in its delights
Life in its revelry

Today the whole horizon
Is a collective grave
Scattered bones

An ossuary
For all to see

A ruin
In its perennial misfortune
In its unchanging fragments

APPARITIONS

Although they seem as wind
They have not left the earth

Although they seem as air
They are old as stone

Like a flock they gather
At the bank of the road

Each one his worry
Each one his poverty

How many ghosts haunt us?
How many wandering souls?

SALON TALK

Everywhere
Conflicting shouts
Threatening gestures

Anger presides over
Our conversations

Rage nourishes
Our encounters

We complain
About the country we live in
About the ills that besiege us

But that's all we do:
Argue until we're tired
Complain without doing anything about it

I have the solution
We scream to one another
But no one puts it into practice
No one puts it to the test

This is the country of those who shout
Just to hear their own voice
To not have to hear what the rest say

El Pozolero[**]

I have lived
To see
Human progress
Dazzling civilization

A bubbling soup
A metal bowl
Caustic soda and bodies dissolving

The thick stew with its stench
Ground zero of culture

[**] El Pozolero is the nickname of Santiago Meza López, a Baja Californian ex-bricklayer. He was arrested in 2009 for disposing of 300 bodies for a gang connected to the Sinaloa cartel. The victims were killed during a dispute between Meza's employer, Teodoro García Semental, and Arellano Félix cartel. Meza dissolved the bodies in caustic soda until they looked like rocks, leaving these remains in ditches. Only three have been discovered, though there may be more. Excavation continues at the three discovered sites: Ojo de Agua, La Gallera and Loma Bonita. The name comes from *pozole*, a kind of meat soup, and is a description of the appearance of bodies dissolving in acid. In Tijuana, bodies of abductees disposed of through chemical means are now referred to as *pozoleados*, "made into soup." (*BBC Mundo*, 22 August 2014)

INDIGNATION

I'm outraged by a country
That only gets outraged
By trivial things

That only protests
In whispers

That doesn't take the time
To take care of itself

I'm outraged
By my own outrage

By my country being
Verses and not deeds

Words
And not lives saved
From the hopelessness
From the slaughter

THE NATIONAL SOUL

In this country nothing changes:
The thirst for blood is the same
The taste for carrion is the same

Our heroes are
Defeat personified

Our villains
Figured out how to take advantage
Of their own betrayals

To devour each other
Is our most dignified conduct
Our best tradition

Urbanism

The *Mondragón* tailor shop is now a Sears
The *Michoacana* diner is now a Dairy Queen
The *Cleopatra* is now a Beauty Supply
La Nacional furniture store is now a Smart and Find
La Española grocery store is now a Best Buy

I'm not complaining:
I'm just stating the obvious

DETECTIVE FICTION

Behind the veil of mist
Fleeting shadows
Vague flashes
Cries of pain

A perfect
Scene of
Noir cinema

Except
This is my country
Not a movie

This
isn't a film set
But my neighborhood every morning

DEAR GOD

Like Paul Celan warned you:
It's time for you to be afraid of us
It's time for you to step aside

Now we feed the hunger of the spirit
Now we give each one his paradise
Now we control your market of rewards and punishments

Accept it
      Dear God:
We turned out better *dealers*
Than you

THE LEECH

The leech is a popular tradition
Say the politicians

The leech is an industry on the rise
Say the businessmen

The leech is a blessing for the country
Say the leaders of public opinion

For the rest of us
The leech is a creature
That feeds on our blood
That grows at the expense of everyone else

Like politicians
Like businessmen
Like leaders of public opinion

The Scene of the Crime

With their new shoes
With their Sunday best
With their work uniform
They all thought they were safe

With a rose in their hair
With the man of their dreams
With the desire to dance all night long
They all thought they were safe

With their painted nails
With their fashionable purses
With their happy personality
They all thought they were safe

In the street with traffic
In the truck they took
In the taxi that they called
They all thought they were safe

None of them noticed
That a shadow was following them
With its instruments of pain
With its knives of horror

And so they disappeared
                    Without a trace
In the burning sands of the desert
Where birds of prey fight
                    For a piece of meat
Where the wolf cleans its snout

With its bloody tongue
With its hunger never satisfied

But they all
—I don't know why: I don't know how—
Thought they were safe in this country of ours

MISSING WOMEN

Their friends say it
Their parents
Their coworkers

They all left without a care
With the moon on their face
With the sun at their backs

Their cousins say it
Their children
Their grandmothers

They all said goodbye with a strong voice,
They all said that they would not be late

Their relatives say it
Their neighbors
Their classmates

They all left the house
And none returned

They all went to parties
And none returned

They all left work
And none returned

They all crossed the threshold
The doorway
The border
Between what they were and what they hoped to be

And none returned

BONES

The bones clamor
To be blood again
The skulls shake
Like grains of sand

What stories do they tell
To those who pass by?
What deaths do they know
To offer them to the world?

Once they had
The future ahead of them
Once they walked
With life awaiting them

Wind unleashed
At the shore of the void
Gusts of time
In its belated shadow

Not even our gaze disturbs them***
Not even our compassion moves them

*** In the original Spanish, the pronoun them in the final verses is the feminine las. However, there is no logical feminine antecedent in the poem. The pronoun must refer to either the title of the poem, osamentas (f. bones), or to the female victims of the preceding poems, which are the same in any case.

Savage Idyll

Between the bushes
In the vacant lots
By the train tracks
Death flaps its wings
Buzzes
                Tears

Flies and blowflies
Maggots and worms
Persistently devour
Whatever they find in their way

The whole world
If necessary

PASTA DE CONCHOS[****]
(IN HOMAGE TO BERTOLT BRECHT)

The politicians I fled
The entrepreneurs I fed
And buried was I
By the king of greed

That was my life:
Running from one place to the other
Trying to escape
Such a fate

I never had the chance
To break my chains:
I was born a prisoner
I died a prisoner

In a tunnel
A thousand meters below the earth

[****] Pasta de Conchos is a coal mine in Coahuila run by Grupo México, the largest mining company in Mexico. On February 19th, 2006 a disaster occurred, leaving 65 dead, 64 widows and 120 children without fathers. To date, only two bodies have been recovered. They were found to have died by asphyxiation. There was no attempt to recover the other bodies. The disaster is considered an "industrial homicide" performed through corruption and negligence. Miners had been complaining of poor conditions in the mine since 2001; the government is accused of accepting money from a corrupt mining union to allow Grupo México to perform "maintenance" in the mine when in reality they were extracting coal. No government official, union worker or Grupo México employee has been brought to trial.

Mexico: I Believe in You

We live in the best of possible worlds
Where the law is a 911 call
That the forces of order never answer

We live in the best possible world
Where the cops give the kids bullets
To play with: so they get used to them

We live in the best possible world
Where students recognize a weapon
By the sound that it makes: by the target it reaches

We live in the best possible world
Where little girls form their own gangs
To dominate their turf: the playground

We live in the best possible world
Where the only way to get ahead
Is to go into business yourself:

Selling drugs in the slums: sex on the street corners
Throwing flares of fire at the face of the world
With anger just beneath your skin: with rage in your fists

CHALK OUTLINES

They've died
They've died in vain

They've died
In the crossfire
Of a war imposed on them
Without asking their permission

Only their kin mourn them
Only old documents preserve
The trace of their lives
The details of their death

They are casualties
In a perennial conflict

Collateral damage
In a country that ignores them

Like wandering ghosts
Their names have been lost

Like witnesses for the prosecution
They are spent ammunition
Burnt powder

HOLOCAUST

Somber
We watch the news

Life is a holocaust
That never stops happening

Every day
One more wound in the side

Every night
A firefight in the middle of the street

The carnival of fear
Besieges us with its shouts
Wraps us in its shroud

NORTHERN BALLAD IN THE STYLE
OF THE BROTHERS GRIMM

At the border
Everything is possible

To be poor
And get rich

To be hated
Until fame comes
And everyone loves you

To be marginalized
And suddenly become
The life of the party

For you to be the one getting beat
And become the one doing the beating
The one that everyone fears

At the border
Fantastic tales
Are a daily occurrence:

The fairy tales
Our gingerbread house
Our oven ready for the cake

VÍCTOR JARA, 1973

You had to see him there
In Chile's national stadium:
A singing prisoner
A wounded bird

You had to see his bruises
His broken ribs
His mutilated tongue

That was his reward
For singing to the people
Of the poor neighborhoods of Santiago

For offering a melody
To those who only expected
Bad weather as their legacy
Destitution as their fate

The soldiers
That only wanted silence
Order and discipline

From Víctor Jara
Only got
The earthen voice of the mines of Chile

The snowy song of its mountains

THE RED WATERS

Now the river doesn't just bring
Fish and logs and trash
Now its waters hold
Bags with drugs
Headless bodies
Useless pistols

Without knowing it
The river
In its murky depths
In its dark whirlpools
Tells our history

The bloody story
      The fateful story
That never finishes bleeding

TIPS FOR BUSINESSMEN

Don't call it a cartel
Call it business

Don't call it crime
Call it commerce

Don't call it a massacre
Call it the free market

Don't call them addicts
Call them customers

Don't call it repression
Call it an insurance policy

You'll find that this way
Everyone will be satisfied
Everyone will invest in your business

Prosperity
Like a singer said
Is a hot gun

A weapon that is pointed gently at your head
And only goes off if there is profit to be had

IN CASE YOU DIDN'T KNOW

It's hardly a secret
Or a revelation

Already E.E. Cummings
Thinking about the disasters
Of his own time
Said it in his own way:

The more dead people there are,
The more alive we feel

The darker the future seems
The more we feel like
Fucking each other

Even at the very end of the world
Life is more voracious than death

THE SEA CEMETERY

Do you remember that officer from the *Kursk*
That wrote his last words
At the bottom of the sea?

Not even the darkness
Kept him from saying what he felt:
He was alive but didn't know
For how much longer

Around him
Everything was sparking
Or creaking in the cold of the irreversible

Regardless
He insisted
On leaving his testimony
So that others would know what happened

We do the same
In this country undone by fear
In this nation by our own hand sunk

BARGAINING

Like a Sunday market
Like a market on wheels
Our country was forged
By trinket-buyers
By dream-sellers

A country that
Changes hands
Like cheap goods

We're always ready
To bargain,
To offer it to the highest bidder

THE ABYSS

The abyss
Is not an open mouth

It is not
Blackness multiplying
Like a virus

The abyss
Is the lack of light
The absence of humanity

Seeing in the neighbor
The enemy
The competitor

The one who isn't like you

THE ETERNAL HOMECOMING

All this chaos grows endlessly
All this craziness continues:
The policemen become thieves
The thieves become politicians
The politicians become pimps
The pimps become bishops
The bishops become judges
The judges become executioners
The executioners become policemen
The policemen become thieves
The thieves become politicians
The politicians become pimps
The pimps become bishops
The bishops become judges
The judges become executioners
The executioners become policemen
The policemen become thieves
The thieves become politicians
The politicians become pimps
The pimps become bishops
The bishops become judges
The judges become executioners
The executioners become policemen
As it is now and ever shall be: always and everywhere

OVERHEARD IN THE STREET

Don't be late
It's looking to be an ugly night
And the wolves are loose

BALANCE

I don't agree with you
Bertolt Brecht:
In times of atrocities
        Speaking about trees
Is not a betrayal of the human spirit

Every flower is a wish
Every trunk is a map
Every branch is a road
Every root is a beginning

And in the distance
The illusion of the landscape

Nature in balance
As vast as a forest
As mysterious as the truth

TRIUMPHAL ANTHEM

Those who march in front
Those who oversee the parade
Those who speak of war in borrowed uniforms
Damn them

Those who shield themselves with the flag
Those who want order at any price
Those who do not know others' pain
Damn them

Those who defend the unforgivable
Those who charge money for applause
Those who do not even accept criticism
Damn them

Those who think themselves pure of spirit
The saviors of the homeland
Those who do not doubt for an instant
Damn them

Birds of prey with their beaks bloodied
Insatiable beasts whose stench fills our days

JEREMIAD

I have never regretted
Having a country like the one I have

What I really regret
Is not having done more
For this babbling country
                              Insecure
That is mine

Not having said: Enough!
When there was still time to save it
When there still remained a fistful of hopes for its future

MOORLAND

The season of year
That we live in
Is the season of uncertainty

The age of chaos
With its sky in pieces

The era of pain
With its emptiness on its back

A moorland burnt
Down to the last root

KIDNAPPERS
(IN THE STYLE OF GERTRUDE STEIN)

If civilization begins
With a rose
There is no other way
To explain how it ends:

A monster is a monster is a monster

IDENTITY

What do I do in this world?
Burn
      Tear
Spit oil on the fire

At every moment
The horror spreads
The fire burns hotter

Fleeing or staying
It doesn't matter

Wherever we go
Mexico is a birthmark
The mark we carry

With defiant poise
With proud impudence

DEFINITIONS

Words define us
They show us just as we are

If I must give a name
To the society in which I live
To the people that I am

I would call it *dog-pack*
I would call us *cruelty*

THE BUCKET

Like Margarite Yourcenar
I carried my bucket of blood
To feed the dead

Only then did the dead turn to look at me
Surprised that the war
That they took part in out of habit
That they all died in
Continued on its course: without end in sight

So many years of poverty
So many gangrened wounds
So many families undone

I told them that that was our punishment

They
The dead
Cried on my shoulder

Like orphans of the homeland that was never ours
Like widows of a land ever thirsty

APPREHENSION

What do people who are afraid talk about?
What language do the mutilated speak?
To what kingdom do the missing belong?

The world is a frontier extending
In all directions

A wall of stone
Ever darker

A barbed-wire fence
Every day higher

We do not fear the future
We fear ourselves

In our own land
We are outsiders

Before the harsh silence
Mistrust separates us
Suspicion unites us

Our country is pure fear:
A noose around our neck
A slit in our throat

DILEMMAS

The dilemma of writing what is happening
Or turning your back on it

The dilemma of living indoors
Or going out into the street

The dilemma of opening your mouth
Or closing it

To keep quiet about what you see
To say what you know

That is the question that arises
Long before taking up the pen
Long before writing the first word

PORTRAIT OF THE HOMELAND

We are country
Half-made
Unfinished
Poorly resolved

A plant
That does not grow
Towards the sun
Or towards the shade

A vine
In a false wall
That does not know
In what direction to grow

Light prematurely aged
Creature perpetually restless

Pablo Neruda Taught Me This

Our duty is to live

Against fear
Against the ashes
Against the executed
Our duty is to live

Against the yokes
Against the chains
Against the murderers
Our duty is to live

Against the threats
Against the extermination
Against the torture rack
Our duty is to live

Against the fatigue
Against the lies
Against the wrongs
Our duty is to live

Against the impunity
Against the intolerance
Against the corrupt
Our duty is to live

Repeat it
As often as necessary:
Our duty is to live

This is our talisman
This our amulet

LANDSCAPE WITH DISASTER AT THE CENTER

Over the mountains
A black cloud

A sudden wind
Raises dust

The clarity becomes clouded
The horizon becomes empty

The dust storm is not
What worries us:
It is the country that moves
Without a fixed path

Its murky whirlpool
Cutting our path

Its noisy avalanche
Falling over us

TODAY

Would you like to hear
The music of fear
The sound of pain?

You can
If you want

In the silence that surrounds you
Just listen carefully
To your own heart: pounding

SELECTIVE MEMORY

In our memory
We burn so many things

The books we read
With fervent passion

The story that gave us
A happy ending
A common identity

Now we go so lightly
Walking through the world

If they asked us who we are
We would not know what to tell them

We would point out to them
                    Perhaps
The three-colored flag
The eagle devouring the serpent

And with our best smile
We would wisely stay silent

A distance
From our own explanation

TERMITES

For this country
That creaks
That shudders

For this country
In precarious balance
What are we?

Its woodworms
Its termites

What undermines
Its foundations

What disintegrates it
Little by little

What gnaws at it
From within

NATIVE-LAND

If there is
Something eternal
In you
I have no idea

If there is
Something miraculous
In you
I do not know it

If I should
Offer proof
Of your holiness
Of your wholeness

I will say
That whales
Journey to your seas

That butterflies
Travel to your forests

That birds sing
At the edge of the water
To be with you

To live with us

WINDMILLS

Before night falls
Before the homeland wilts
Does anyone wish to speak in its favor?

We have given and received
An inheritance of blood
For too long

We have grown
Under the sonorous roar of cannons
In the heroic battle against what is unjust

But injustice is still with us
The triumphs have been false
The victories
                    Ephemeral

Every generation
Has had to fight
Similar battles
Exhausting struggles
Against the same terrors

It is time
To rethink
All of our history

To bet
On a country
With open doors

A homeland that works
Without executioners in sight
Without victims of convenience

Where no one humiliates you
Insults you
Kills you

Where no one worships
Any glory
Other than his own convictions

The tangle of the imperfect
The joy of adventure

WALKING WITH HERMANN BROCH
THROUGH THE VILLAGE OF COMALA^{*****}

Why must you write poetry?
Hermann Broch asks me
And then answers himself:
To proclaim all of our infamies

There are too many of them
I answer him

The master is undaunted
By my disdainful reply:
Speak then of all of them
Because each one
Is a nuance of our
Unbearable martyrdom

Around us
The tolling of bells and alleluias
War like a vulgar spectacle
Like a parade of executioners
Like an altar of sacrifice

Hermann Broch does not give up:
Have the courage to call unworthy what is unworthy
Have the honesty to call victims victims

What is the use?
I ask him
His words buzz in my ears
It is useful

***** Comala is a town of ghosts, as told by Juan Rulfo in his famous novel *Pedro Páramo* (1955). Common grave in the collective memory. Hell to our measure and likeness.

For it helps others
Not to fall into the abyss
So that others
In the future
Can flee blood and torture
Their monstrous proliferation

The cars pass us by
With their stereos at full blast
People walk without looking each other in the face:
Each one his trench
Every one an impregnable fortress

Broch studies them with care
Before giving his verdict:
They live in the bewitched cauldron
In abstract negligence
Their knowledge was turned into vain senselessness
They believe that the only way out
Is to trample their fellows
To hurt their neighbors
As long as they are not hurt

What do you expect them to do?
I reply
They are on their way to the gallows

No!
Says Broch
With an expression of pain
They are returning from them: they are dead and yet live

At the outskirts of the village
We say goodbye

Hermann Broch looks into my eyes
With his crow-like gaze:
Do not prize death
Do not praise the unworthy
They must no longer be blind in face of what is germinating

And turning his back to me
He leaves in a hurry:
A shadow that takes flight
A black dot among the whiteness of our scattered bones

GREAT FLOOD

The clouds close all the exits
The sky has become impenetrable

Everywhere
Lightning bolts burst

The rain is a prophecy fulfilled
A prologue to the calamity
That awaits us

Nervous
The doves fly and hide

I don't lose sight of them:
In their beaks they must bring
An olive branch

The promise of a new world
Of a newborn earth

VISION

Above the ruins of my country
I see a shooting star
A dazzling aster

For an instant
That vision seemed
The crystallization of all our wishes

A breath of hope
Able to lift a people
Out of its fears: out of its betrayals

A happy promise
To give confidence to the hopeless
Healing to the wounded

Above the ruins of my country
There are still roads to travel
Horizons with dawn as a destination

With light
As an ending

POETICS

Give a name
To everything
That interests you

Give life
To every being
You come across

What you see
What you touch
What you experience

Poetry has worth
Because of what it touches
Because of what it gathers up

PARTNER

For Karla

In the evening
Suddenly
        Silence

The calm
In the eye
Of the storm

Without charging armies
Without war cries
The heart rests

The world
Is no longer
A suit of armor
But dream water

The pulse
With which life
Unites us

With which love feeds us

Villagers

My way of life smells of a village
Wislawa Szymborska

We live at the edge of time
At the northernmost border
We live in a minor province of the great empire

Even the tax collectors
Barely visit us

Our history
Is a footnote

No one counts on us
At the celebrations of the kingdom

The learned say
That nothing important
Has happened here

That the decisive battles
Never took place
In our village

We are
–As an ancient poet said–
Poorly prepared for honors
Our way of life does not smell like a royal palace
But like a simple village

If there are bloody victories
If there are triumphant armies
We had nothing to do with them

While others were seeking
Glory or power
We were watering the earth
So that it would yield splendid harvests
Or we were playing with are children
Or we were making love to our women

We never tried to be
Anything other than what we are:
Border people by tradition
Villagers by birth

SONG TO CHEER ON THE PARADE

Call my homeland
Pain
Call its legacy
Betrayal

If we are its children
What bad luck
If we are its executioners
What a disgrace

German Idealism (Mexican Version)

We are not demigods
Or harmless creatures

The world burns
Because we
Its fire feed

Beauty
We like
Dressed in blood

Pain
Moves us
Through pure fantasy

The moral high ground
The lofty will
Are our ideals

Brute force
The only law with substance

If someone does not obey
Crush him!

DEBITS

We need a way out
A heart without darkness at its bottom

We need an outstretched hand
When all seems lost

An omen
To be fulfilled
In the face of darkness afoot

A melody
To be sung
Without fear in our eyes

Post Card Sent to Myself

The brown sky
        Yellowish
With its flaming air

The horizon
With its cloud of flies
And its marks of poverty

In the abandoned houses
Love shacks

In the empty lots
Dismembered corpses

On the medians
Drug dealers
Fire swallowers

At the end of the square
The children play
Unaware of their surroundings

This is my country
In its hardness
This is my homeland
In its tenderness

STONE SOUP

Mineral soup
With water its only juice
With absence its only meat

Soup of the poor people
Who trick themselves
With a bit of hot liquid
With the steam of unfulfilled promises

Nothing soup
To drink at any hour
To savor with one's eyes closed

This is our daily meal
This our sustenance

THE BANQUET OF TIME

It is not the great bread of transcendence
That I seek

I seek the pieces of the world
In its lost unity

I look for its crumbs
After the banquet

Amorphous pieces
In their cold-hearted beauty

Dust of light
Constantly wearing away

What the Conquistadors Left Us

Shreds of sails
        Broken helmets
Timbers rotting in the sun
Down to their last splinter
Rusty swords
        With no edge
But a briny crust

That is all the salvage
That is what time saves
Centuries later
When nothing is left
of the conquistadors
Not even a shadow to shelter them
Nor a tomb worthy of the name

They came in search of dreams
And ended up turning into
A empire vanished
Into the incomprehensible sands

A pack of ghosts
That the wind covers with dust

Runaway horsemen
That never returned home

A spark
                        Barely
On the horizon of history

A grain of salt
In the planet's supply

WHEEL OF FORTUNE

To every time its maladies
To every memory its remains

The world is a cry of terror
In an empty square

Memory burning
Until all that is left
Is the soot on the walls

The timely darkness

THE CRIME SCENE

Broken bottles
The smell of beer

Spent shells on the floor
Inert bodies

The chaos
Of blood
Being spilt

The sticky
Presence
Of death

Its reddened pupil
Its indelible insanity

POETIC ENCOUNTER

The man
Almost apologetically
Approaches my table

I sell poems
He says

Verses
Barely readable
On photocopied pages

Are they yours?
I ask

No
He answers
Bowing his head:
They are everyone's

FACEBOOK

In homage to Henri Michaux

As a kid I had
Three or four friends
Few but enough
To share the bike
To fly the kite
To play hide-and-seek

Years later
I logged in to Facebook
And I had a hundred friends
No: a thousand friends
No: ten thousand friends

Now
I would I could have
Three or four friends once again
Like the ones I had as a kid

The ones that are worth it
The ones that never go away

Signs

Every word is a return
To one's birth country: a living
Under the frond
Of a tongue that does not know drought

Every word is a story
Rising in the night
To not be lost in oblivion

A river bathing
The shores of time
With its waters

An eternal sky, gold in the evening

HESITATION

Rockslide
The fault that opens
At our feet

In a moment
The world separates

What do we hold on to
When nothing is secure?

Who do we call
For help
From the unease?

The ground trembles
Without respite

It is useless to complain:
Although the sky may fall
This is our home

A tightrope
An act of grace

THE MORAL

Do not be afraid:
The body is birth
Always: everywhere.

SHOUT OF WARNING

Although it may seem that way
The poem refrains from saying it all
From giving each thing its true name

The poem is a parchment
That tells the saga
Of the world in detail

A tomb recently discovered
Beneath the dust of the desert

Although it may never admit it
The poem is the dark side
Of nature

A trail of blood
In daylight

A shout of warning
In the middle of disaster

The light that journeys on its own and at its own risk
The fire that gives life to what it burns

Word by word
Silence after silence

AT HOME

The water is lovelier as it goes over a cliff
Ricardo Flores Magón

Sometimes we forget that there are other worlds
Other faces marked by identical storms
Other rivers that slither toward a common sea:
Toward the final frontier

Sometimes we think like a Mobius strip: returning
To the same ideas: repeating the same words as always
To feel safe: at home: with our loved ones

Sometimes: however: the walls fall: the routines are broken
And the world that belongs to us falls to pieces: it becomes a fire
Made of ashes and calamities: of senseless cries

Sometimes only our gazes stay upright
Our eyes that look beyond the wooden fence
Beyond the known world where maps disregard its boundaries

Those other worlds that in the end we travel with uncertain steps
Those other shires that offer us their landscapes
Those other lives so different: so similar to ours

Sometimes we only need to make a memory: to raise our eyes
So that the world is an open window: waiting for us
A dialogue of light in the house of air: a crossing with its
        destination on its back

A trail of illusions after their baptism

MEXICO, 1935

You are Old Mexico
Rafael Alberti

We are what you saw
      Rafael
A land of cacti and agaves
Where time tires
Of counting the changes of seasons
The curves of the sky

We are a mural painted
With bright colors
So that tourists believe
That Mexico is Indians with serpents' eyes

But at the end of your wanderings
      Rafael
You learned that this land
Where the grass grows
In the shadow of the pyramids
Is populated by hungry gods

By wandering souls
That cross the fields
With firelight in their eyes
And burning coals for a flag

We are a race
Born in the shaking of the earth
In the clamor of sacrifice
In the dryness of the air

A people
That makes of pain a dance
Of death a smile

A community
That does not retreat
Before the gales: the abuses: the affronts

Land of porcupines and dragonflies
Of mockingbirds and fighting cocks

Land chained
To its deepest roots
To the shortest-lived deities
To the song that is sung
From the voice of the thistles
From the light of the disaster

Dark blood
In its sharp thwack
In its life in embers

Petrified sun
With its long shadow of an unmoving lizard
With its gunpowder about to explode in our face

AFTERSHOCKS

The city spins: a windmill in which everything comes undone
Angel González

The earth moves at its own rhythm
It shakes our nonchalance at least once a day
With each of its movements
It awakes in us the conscience of uncertainty

The earth is an exemplary teacher
When it teaches us to notice what we are:
Remoras of a terrible monster
In whose shadow we live, expecting

The earth is a cracked horizon
A fissure that is the owner of its own void
Its loveliness is pure panic
Its strength a collective cry

The earth is a surprising substance
Like the sea in its sudden tide
In her there is no unity but asymmetry
There is no absolute but difference

The earth at our feet now sounds
Like the trumpet of the apocalypse:
Music of living fire: of sliding rock
That with its roar smashes our trust to pieces

Nature created with harsh storms
Born of unfathomable spasms
That throws our gestures of arrogance to the ground
Our masks as kings of progress

And leaves in its place dust in the wind
The rubble in its broken beauty
Deserted paradise where only the light
Subsists in its tomb: death without pause or rest

Like a dance of frights in the endless night
Like a nightmare revolving over the earth

JAPAN, 2011

Someone should tell the world:
You are broken

Like a vase
Smashed to pieces
Irreparable

And all that remains
Is the memory of better times

The fragments
Of a sun
Being born among the waters

TRENCHES

The Wall of China
Hadrian's Wall
The Maginot Line
They are useless boundaries
That did not achieve their purpose:
To hinder the passage of the enemy
To stop the invaders of the empire
To keep the barbarians at bay
The savages with their harsh cries

We
Who see their walls demolished
Their dry ditches
Their trenches filled with wild grass
We know it well

We
The heirs of the barbarians
The descendants of the savages
We are the final moral of the borders

The living symbol of their greatest failure

White Light

Speak: say it: this light
Is a deep sigh
In the bonfire of time

A scratch of the sun
On the veil of the world

A window
Open to the things that tremble
In the fade-out of the air

Know it from here on:
The sky shines anywhere
The earth burns for us

SPRING

Do you feel it already?
Do you notice its presence?

Days of March
Winds of April

Spring returns
With its proud openness

At the shore of the river
New flowers

In the middle of the field
The nuptial flight

ARCADIA

Don't come to tell us
That history is the future
In its faraway dawn
The light in its holocaust
The earth in its seed

We already know that

We are the breath of the things to come
Of the beings to be born

A wishing well
Where time makes its way
To the first word: to the last seed

Arcadia we call
The sky of stars that shine
The way towards the lap of life

That season when the sun lasts in its offerings
That age that gives us its gesture of solidarity

Its gift
In front of death
Who smiles

THE BEST WAY

You're right
                    Kenneth Patchen
The best way to build a house
Is to build it
To adjust and measure
So that the materials fit together
To sticking together and repairing
Until the walls are raised
Until the roofs serve
As a refuge for the doves
And life nests between the tiles
With its cheep of a newborn chick

You're right
                    Kenneth Patchen
The best way to write a poem
Is to write it
So that the words work at their own pace
So that the verse chooses its own path

Like an act of love
Like a sanctuary open to whoever needs it

*E*very day someone writes about their country. There are so many reasons to complain, so many things going wrong, so many obvious abuses from any point of view. I decided to reflect on México as an act of public consciousness, as a demand for clarity on behalf of the country that we have spoiled with our eyes shut. As much as I looked for a poetry that would touch a raw nerve—when I began to write about the state of the Mexican nation in 2010, 2011—I could not find works of poetry that would reference the catastrophic situation in which we lived then and in which we continue to live now.

I wanted a poetry that would look the world in the eyes, with no tricks, no excuses. That the poem is not another reality, just this one, the one we are suffering through its gales and complaints. That the verse be a radical cure, a purifying incantation. For what purpose? To give voice to the common pain, to the hardship of a community shocked by bloodshed, by the impunity of the powerful, by unrestrained disputes.

Because poetry is also a public arena where complaints and abuses have a place, where resentments and tragedies can be heard. That the poetic word is not alien to our here and now, nor does it shy away from saying things by name. The texts that are part of Civil Poems were born from there, from that desperation and agony. They are observations on the fly of a country immersed in a growing violence that expands through all parts of the social body. They are life drawings of the daily horror, of the feelings shared by Mexicans on their bloody journey. Because poetry, to be a vital instrument, should first and foremost be honest with itself, should demonstrate what it is made of with emotion and challenge, as truth made flesh and bone.

Civil Poems was published in Spain in 2013 by Amargord Press and it is, I admit, a work created under the dark shadow of the war against the drug cartels. It is neither a disaster diary nor protest poetry, although it has some of both. It is, above all, the life of the people in verse, the song of the hopeless written by one more witness. Why deny it? México pains me, like it pains so many. What Civil Poems expresses, through themes and perspectives, is the mixture of conflicting emotions that we, as a society and as individuals, feel at an overwhelming moment of our history, when community ties are breaking and all we have left as a last resort is everyone for themselves. It is not a glorious moment for anyone. It is not a time that will make us proud to have been part of. But poetry is an art exceedingly gifted and prepared to face difficult times, to explore the evils that overwhelm us. That is what I have attempted to do in this work.

To apprehend, using free verse, the emotional states and deficiencies that we suffer and that have led us to live like we live, to die like we die. There is so much brutality, so much blindness surrounding us, that poetry can barely raise its voice amongst the unrestrained screams of the victims and the executioners, amongst the participants in the march toward all that is sinister, toward the carnival of the macabre. I wrote these poems because I do not accept the normalcy of violence, the charade of impunity, the pretext of ignorance. I wrote them to say what I think and what I feel as a Mexican in a nation that is falling apart day by day, where inequality and injustice are growing by leaps and bounds and with the permission of those who have the most. I did not want it be a collection of political poetry but of human poetry. Civil Poems is my way of reclaiming the right to say what I am in the middle of a calamity that we are all responsible for, of a disaster that displays our signature, that bears our likeness, that defines our culture. Nonetheless, the tone of the poems began to change toward the end of the collection. The poems that conclude the book began to be filled with light, with vitality, with a certain enthusiasm. That desire to not lose hope became stronger.

Civil Poems may be read in many ways: As a house with its darkened rooms and luminous bedrooms, with windows wide open and basements full of darkness; a place where words serve to heal our wounds and the verse is "an act of love," "a sanctuary open to whomever needs it." I do not know nor do I care if it is in the style of current Mexican poetry, so conservative, so prudent so that it does not show what it really thinks of the world. I decided to say what I think, what I feel, what makes my stomach turn, what affects me here and now. To move the waters so that the filth does not settle. To call things by their name so that no one tells me that I lived this moment in history as a volunteer executioner, as an absent witness.

That is poetry for me: An ID, a public text. Something that you expel in order to not choke on your own bile. Something you should say so as to not betray the words that belong to you, the language that you have in your care. A full-body portrait of my homeland in all its catastrophes, of the world in its disasters. And now, thanks to the generous work of José María Mantero and with the support of Phillip Dunn, these verses are present in the English language, in that language that William Shakespeare would use to speak of a nation that groans beneath the imperious ruin, of a world "of graves, of worms, and epitaphs," where death has its kingdom and oblivion is the absolute monarch. Because poetry knows no borders. Because poetry shares with all of us its words of hope, its testimonies of pain. That which unites every one of us in time and place. That which drives us forward to continue living our surroundings to sing its dreams, its anxieties, its certainties. That which terrorizes and delights us. That which fortifies and dignifies us. It is what calls us to keep going, to despair not. A mirage defended and treasured by the heart. A utopia that is never at peace.

Gabriel Trujillo Muñoz (Mexicali, Mexico, 1958). Poet, essayist and novelist, lives on the Mexican border with the United States. He was one of the founders of Binational Press (1987-1996) and New Borders (2014 to date), projects that have sought to illuminate art and literature from both sides of the international line. He is the author of Historical, Detective, Fantasy and Science Fiction novels, many of which take place on the border. As an essayist, he has been concerned with studying the artistic manifestations of his region. As a poet, his main themes have been the exploration of the frontier as a home of mirages and wonders, the inquiry of the desert as a sacred zone and the recounting of his personal past as truthful mirror of his time and circumstance. Some of his books of poetry are *Perceptions* (1983), *After the Mirage* (1989), *In Broad Daylight* (1992), *Gift of Tongues* (1995), *Constellations* (1997), *Stubble* (2001), *Bordertown* (2006), *Boundaries* (2007), *Civil Poems* (2013), *Lights on* (2016), *Periphery* (2016) and *Out of Order* (2018). The San Diego University Press published *Permanent Work* (1993), an anthology of his poetry. He is a member of the Mexican Academy of the Language since 2011.

www.ingramcontent.com/pod-product-compliance
Lightning Source LLC
Chambersburg PA
CBHW011216120626
46545CB00008B/3013